MW01492373

THE SECRET, MYSTIFYING, UNUSUAL HISTORY OF Magic

BY PATRICE SHERMAN

Content Consultant: Scott Penrose
Curator, The Magic Circle Museum
London, England

CAPSTONE PRESS
a capstone imprint

Velocity is published by Capstone Press,
151 Good Counsel Drive, P.O. Box 669, Mankato, Minnesota 56002.
www.capstonepub.com

032010
005741WZF10

Books published by Capstone Press are manufactured with paper containing at least 10 percent post-consumer waste.

Library of Congress Cataloging-in-Publication Data
Sherman, Patrice.
 The secret, mystifying, unusual history of magic / by Patrice Sherman.
  p. cm.—(Velocity. Unusual histories)
 Includes bibliographical references and index.
 Summary: "Describes the history of magicians and performance magic, featuring little known facts and bizarre inside information"—Provided by publisher.
 ISBN 978-1-4296-4791-5 (library binding)
 1. Magic tricks—History—Juvenile literature. 2. Magicians—History—Juvenile literature. I. Title. II. Series.
 GV1548.S495 2011
 793.8—dc22   2010012357

Editorial Credits
Editor: Jenny Marks
Designers: Veronica Correia and Ashlee Suker
Media Researcher: Wanda Winch
Production Specialist: Eric Manske

Photo Credits
Alamy: Interfoto, 12 (bottom), Mary Evans Picture Library, 23 (top), The Protected Art Archive, 32 (left); AP Images: Ray Stubblebine, 27 (bottom); The Bridgeman Art Library International: Stapleton Collection/Private Collection/Evelyn Paul, 5 (top); Capstone: 38 (bottom); Corbis: 36 (top), Bettmann, 33, Star Ledger/Jennifer Brown, 41 (bottom), Sygma/Tony Korody, 38 (top); Courtesy of Lance Burton, 31 (bottom); Courtesy of Michael Claxton, Ph.D., 36 (bottom left); Courtesy of the Todd Karr Collection, 14, 17 (middle); Getty Images: AFP/Timothy A. Clary, 40 (bottom), Hulton Archive, 34 (top), Matthew Peyton, 42, Museum of the City of New York/Byron Collection, 27 (top), NY Daily News Archive/George Schmidt, 26, Time Life Pictures/Alan Levenson, cover, Time Life Pictures/Mansell, 22 (Houdini escape sequence); The Granger Collection, New York, 9 (bottom right); International Brotherhood of Magicians, 37 (bottom), 45 (bottom); iStockphoto: Barbara Sauder, 17 (top left), Elisabeth Perotin, 8, 44 (top), Rakoskerti, 17 (top right); Joe Putrock, 43 (bottom); Library of Congress: Prints and Photographs Division, 9 (top right), 21 (middle right), 23 (bottom), 24 (all), 25 (bottom), 31 (top), 45 (top); Newscom, 9 (left), AFP, 6; Shutterstock: Adisa, 39 (top), Alexia Khruscheva, 11, Antonov Roman, 22 (razor blade), Anyka, 29 (right), Awe Inspiring Images, 43 (top), basel101658, 10 (back), Bob Orsillo, 37 (top), Chas, 4 (goose), Chris Fisher, 25 (back), Craig Hill, 39 (front), Dario Sabljak, 34 (bottom), Digital N, 40 (top left), Digital Studio, 26-27 (back), Dr. Den, 18 (top), 19 (bottom), Dr. Le Thanh Hung, 20 (bottom), Eric Isselee, 35 (tiger), Hintau Aliaskei, 18 (torn paper background), 19 (back), 31 (back), iofoto, 37 (middle), Irina Tischenko, 14 (back), 15 (bottom), 44 (bottom), Ivan Ponomarev, 30 (top), Jens Stolt, 17 (bottom), Jim Barber, 10 (left), Jlqf, 16-17 (wood), John Lock, 36-37 (butterflies), Joshua Haviv, 39 (skyline), Katrina Brown, 15 (top), 44 (bottom), Kiselev Andrey Valerevich, 30 (bottom), l. Quintanilla, 10 (right), Laurie K, 22 (bobby pins), leifr, 40 (top right), lymsts, 41 (cap), Marlene Greene, 20 (top), Matt Valentine, 19 (middle bullet), Maugli, background design used on cover and throughout book, maxstockphoto, 36 (frame), Mikhail, 7, Mindy w.m. Chung, 16 (top), Neo Edmund, 20-21 (wood background), Olemac, 16 (bottom), Picsfive, 32 (right), Richard Laschon, 12-13 (map), Robert Taylor, 29 (left), Robyn Mackenzie, 23-25 (photo frame), Stephen Mulcahey, 36 (bottom right), stishok, 28, Svetlana Mikhalevich, 18-19 (fiber background), Valentin Agapov, 21 (frame), Vlue, 18-19 (middle guns), 35 (jeans), Warren Parsons, 18 (bottom), Wolfgang Amri, 35 (t-shirt), Yellowj, 21 (top left), Yuri Arcurs, 41 (python); Wikipedia/Keith Schengili-Roberts, 4-5 (bottom)

TABLE OF CONTENTS

Chapter 1

Sorcery and Sleight of Hand

Early Magic and Magicians

Dedi: The Pharaoh's Magician

About 5,000 years ago in ancient Egypt, the pharoah Cheops learned of an amazing sorcerer named Dedi. People claimed Dedi could cut off a man's head and reattach it, good as new. The pharoah insisted the sorcerer be brought to him to perform this feat.

According to legend, when Dedi arrived at the pharaoh's court, he shook his head. No, he said, he would not perform his magic on a man. But he could perform it on a goose.

After beheading the live bird, Dedi placed the body at one end of the pharaoh's throne room and the head at the other. As Dedi chanted a spell, the goose's head and body rejoined. The goose started honking and flapping its wings. It was alive again!

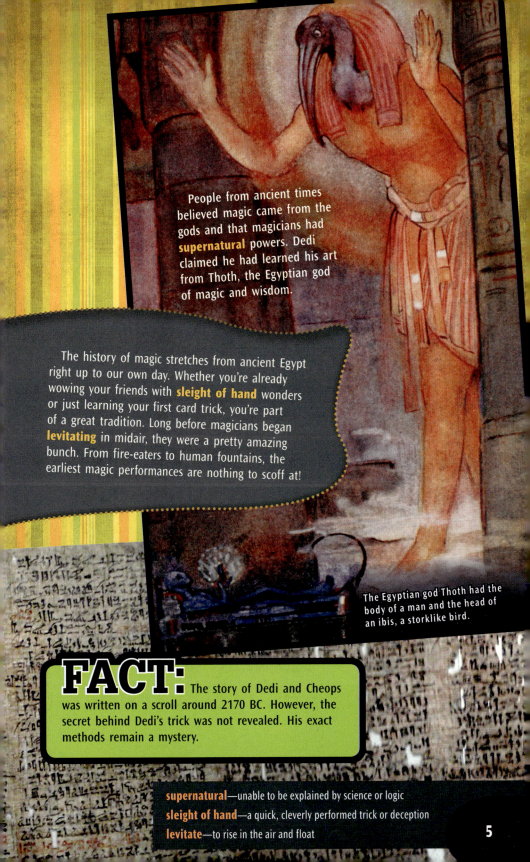

People from ancient times believed magic came from the gods and that magicians had **supernatural** powers. Dedi claimed he had learned his art from Thoth, the Egyptian god of magic and wisdom.

The history of magic stretches from ancient Egypt right up to our own day. Whether you're already wowing your friends with **sleight of hand** wonders or just learning your first card trick, you're part of a great tradition. Long before magicians began **levitating** in midair, they were a pretty amazing bunch. From fire-eaters to human fountains, the earliest magic performances are nothing to scoff at!

The Egyptian god Thoth had the body of a man and the head of an ibis, a storklike bird.

FACT:
The story of Dedi and Cheops was written on a scroll around 2170 BC. However, the secret behind Dedi's trick was not revealed. His exact methods remain a mystery.

supernatural—unable to be explained by science or logic
sleight of hand—a quick, cleverly performed trick or deception
levitate—to rise in the air and float

Ancient Fire Breathers

In 135 BC, a Syrian soldier and magician named Eunios frightened his enemies with his blazing breath. But the fire never touched his lips. How did he do it?

FACT: Today's fire breathers rely on flammable liquids like kerosene to create a flame.

Eunios' Flame-Blowing Trick Revealed!

1. First, Eunios drilled two holes at the ends of a hollowed nut.

2. He filled the nut with oil and sulfur.

3. Then Eunios hid the nut in his mouth between his teeth.

4. Using a piece of burning ember, Eunios lit the outer end of the nut and waited until the liquid mixure inside caught fire.

5. Gently, he blew flames out the hole.

Mountebanks and Juggling Monks

During the Middle Ages (400–1350) and Renaissance (1350–1600), magicians performed at fairs and festivals throughout Europe. In 1133, an English monk and juggler, Rahere, started a fair in London, England, to celebrate St. Bartholomew's Day. Every year on August 24th, crowds gathered to eat, dance, and be merry. Acrobats, jugglers, and magicians provided entertainment.

Magicians, called mountebanks, performed on stages made of boards laid across two simple, wooden frames.

Mountebanks dressed in long robes embroidered with moons and stars.

Their **conjuring** tricks included sword swallowing and fire-eating.

conjure—to do something by magic

The Magic Wardrobe

The typical magician's attire has changed many times since magic got its start in ancient Egypt. Popular trends often alternate between elaborate, caped costumes and simple, no-frills street clothes.

In the 1800s, Robert-Houdin changed the look of magic. He was one of the first to don a black suit for performances.

In the Middle Ages, mountebanks performed wearing flowing robes with stars.

Modern-day magician Criss Angel looks more like a rock star than a wizard.

Straight from the Magician's Mouth

Another trick loved by Renaissance fair-goers was the "human fountain." A magician swallowed a pitcher full of water, then spit it out in arcs of red, pink, orange, blue, and green. Some could spit several different-colored streams at once.

How was it done?
Before the performance, the magician tucked a few small sacks of pre-tinted water in his mouth. During the show, he simply swallowed the clear water, and then bit down on the sacks to become a multi-colored human fountain.

In the 1600s, fairgoers in England were astounded by William Banks and his performing horse, Marocco. Marocco's act included dancing, picking people out of a crowd, and counting money with his hooves. How? Banks gave him secret signals to start and stop tapping. But the crowds thought it must be magic!

4

3

2

1

FACT: Marocco was so well known that he even appears in classic literature. Shakespeare mentioned "the dancing horse" in his play, *Love's Labour's Lost*. Most believe this horse was Marocco.

Take a Magical Mystery Tour with The Cups and Balls

If you landed in the Lower East Side of **New York** around 1910, you'd find street hustlers from Ireland, Russia, Poland, Italy, Greece, Syria, and a dozen other countries. Many hustlers played a variation of The Cups and Balls with three walnut shells and a dried pea. They might ask you to bet a buffalo nickel to guess which shell the pea was under. (A nickel could get you a hot dog on Coney Island in those days!)

Seneca the Younger

The Cups and Balls is one of the oldest magic tricks in the world. Using three cups and three small balls, the magician makes the balls disappear, change shape and size, or even turn into a live chick or mouse.

The earliest known written reference to The Cups and Balls is in a letter written by Seneca the Younger, a Roman philosopher (4 BC–AD 65).

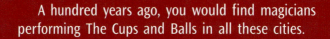

A hundred years ago, you would find magicians performing The Cups and Balls in all these cities.

In **London,** you might see a mountebank standing behind a tall table and performing with brass cups and cork balls.

In **Munich,** you'd find *taschenspielers* carrying their cups and balls in little bags tied to their waists. The German name for The Cups and Balls is *das Becherspiel*, meaning "the cup game" or "the cup trick."

In **Paris**, you'd see *escamoteurs* using coffee cups and balls of wadded up paper.

In **New Delhi**, magicians called *fakirs* used bell-like wooden bowls topped with handles. Their bright cloth balls were made of cotton.

In **Venice,** you could watch a *giocatore di bussolotti* performing a *bussolotto* trick using a dice cup.

Chapter 2

Jean Eugene Robert-Houdin

Father of Modern Magic

The Accidental Magician

Born in Blois, France, in 1805, Jean Eugene Robert-Houdin wanted to be a watchmaker like his father. In his early 20s, Robert-Houdin ordered a set of books on watchmaking from a local bookseller.

Imagine Robert-Houdin's surprise when he mistakenly received books on magic tricks. But instead of returning the books, he read them cover to cover. In fact, he memorized them. Soon he began performing for his friends.

In the 1830s, Robert-Houdin moved to Paris to become a professional magician. His skills as a watchmaker proved useful too, for he could also construct mechanical figures called **automatons**.

Clockwork automatons worked by secret pulleys and levers. They could write, dance, and even play musical instruments.

Robert-Houdin sold automatons to other performers and used them in his own acts.

an automaton

Robert-Houdin

automaton—a robot or mechanical figure made to resemble a person or animal

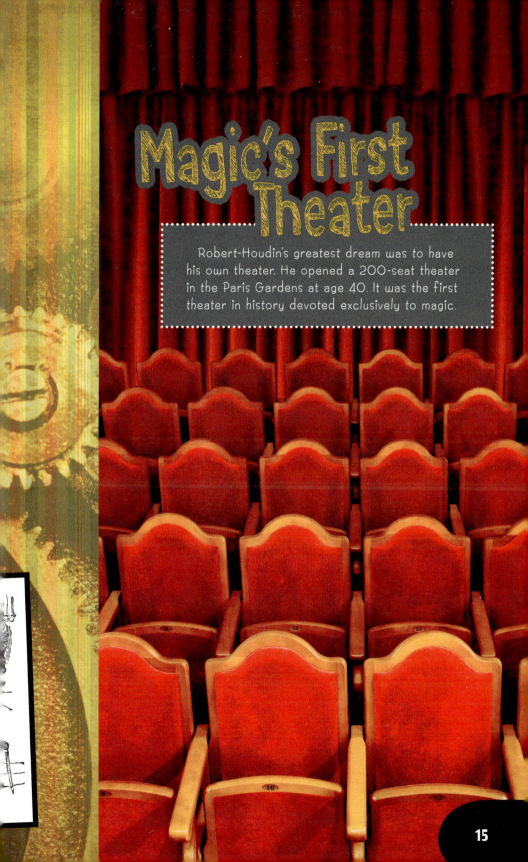

Magic's First Theater

Robert-Houdin's greatest dream was to have his own theater. He opened a 200-seat theater in the Paris Gardens at age 40. It was the first theater in history devoted exclusively to magic.

The Mystery of Second Sight

Robert-Houdin trained his son Emile to become a magician too. Emile proved an excellent student. In 1846, when Emile was 14, Robert-Houdin introduced an act he billed as "Second Sight."

Emile sat onstage blindfolded. Meanwhile, Robert-Houdin silently collected small personal objects from the spectators. Then he would ask Emile to describe what he was holding. Without fail, Emile would describe the object and the person who had lent it.

Emile became such an expert "mind reader" that he could identify hundreds of items. To do this, he memorized a code of thousands of words and phrases. For example, Robert-Houdin may have used the phrase "What do I hold in my hand?" This might tell Emile that Robert-Houdin was holding a pair of glasses.

FACT:

Jean Eugene Robert-Houdin died on June 13, 1871. Today, the *Maison de la Magie,* his former home in Blois, France, is a museum devoted to his art and life.

Emile's magical powers of second sight were only a clever trick. But the use of this code is a demonstration of dedication and great skill.

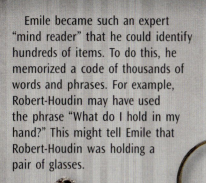

Emile's father, Jean Eugene Robert-Houdin, holds an audience member's item.

Blindfolded Emile Robert-Houdin describes the item.

Magic's Most Deadly Trick

As the theater falls silent, magicians Penn Jillette and Raymond Teller walk to opposite sides of the stage, each holding a loaded gun. They turn toward each other. "Ready, aim, fire!" an assistant calls out. The guns go off together.

A moment later, each magician spits out a mashed up bullet, previously marked by a member of the audience with his or her initials. Are the bullets authentic? Experts examine them. Yes, they are. Did the guns really fire them? Again, the experts say yes.

So how did Penn and Teller manage to catch one another's bullets in their teeth and live? The Bullet Catch is magic's most dangerous trick. At least 12 magicians have died while performing it, and many others have been injured.

How does it work? Some believe that an assistant somehow manages to copy the initials onto two mashed-up bullets and slip the right bullet to the right magician while they are donning their bullet-proof vests. This would have to be done very swiftly so that no one else would see what was going on. Another theory is that the bullets are secretly replaced by wax slugs with hardened shells. Once fired, the wax melts and the mashed shell appears to be like that of a genuine bullet.

What do the magicians say? Teller's not telling, and neither is Penn. The stunt, however, continues to thrill spectators.

1,000 feet per second

FACT: Chung Ling Soo
and H. T. Sartell are two notable magicians who died attempting the dangerous bullet catch trick. In Sartell's case, his wife assisted him with the bullet catch and used real bullets in the pistol. Did she do it deliberately? No one knows.

Chapter 3

Houdini and His Great Escapes

America's Immigrant Magician

Many people think that Eric Weiss was the greatest magician ever. Eric who? **Houdini**, that's who!

Eric Weiss was born in Hungary in 1874. He came to America at the age of 4. His family couldn't afford to send him to school, so he took odd jobs helping shopkeepers and selling newspapers on the street. But Weiss never did anything the ordinary way. To attract customers, he performed acrobatics and magic tricks he had learned from a book. By his late teens, he knew he could earn more money as a magician than he did as a salesman.

Hungary, the birthplace of Houdini

Weiss knew he needed a new name if he wanted to succeed as a magician—something that people would remember. He had just read the story of Robert-Houdin's life. Out of admiration for the French magician, Weiss changed his name to Harry Houdini. He vowed that one day he would be even greater than Robert-Houdin.

FACT: America's first recorded magician was born in Boston, Massachusetts, in 1783. Richard Potter started his own traveling magic show in 1811. He could perform more than 100 different tricks.

The Escape Artist

Houdini was strong, flexible, and athletic. He trained to hold his breath for long periods of time. He taught himself to squeeze into smaller and smaller spaces. He practiced expanding and contracting his muscles to slip out of chains, handcuffs, and ropes.

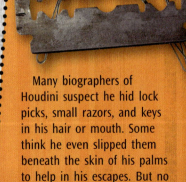

Many biographers of Houdini suspect he hid lock picks, small razors, and keys in his hair or mouth. Some think he even slipped them beneath the skin of his palms to help in his escapes. But no one knows for sure. Houdini kept his methods secret.

In New York, Houdini had himself suspended upside down from a skyscraper while buckled in a **straitjacket**. Traffic in the city came to a dead halt while crowds watched Houdini twist and turn. Finally, he managed to break free.

FACT:

The Needle Trick was another of Houdini's most famous. After swallowing dozens of needles and thread, Houdini retrieved the string with all the needles neatly threaded.

straitjacket—a jacket with long sleeves that can be tied behind the wearer's back as a form of restraint

Torture, Milk Cans, and Coffins

During stage performances, Houdini was bound with chains and stuffed into a large, metal milk can. Assistants then filled the can with water and sealed it tightly. Houdini could hold his breath for three minutes or more to escape from the can. Sometimes Houdini asked a spectator to hold his or her breath along with him. The average person gave up after a mere 30 seconds.

Houdini also had himself suspended upside down in a glass tank filled with water. This most famous of his escapes was called The Water Torture Cell. On another occasion, he was buried alive in a sealed casket beneath 7 feet (2 meters) of sand. Many of Houdini's escapes were so clever that, even today, no one knows how he did them.

On July 7, 1912 Houdini was **manacled** and placed inside a wooden box. Nailed shut and weighted with 200 pounds (91 kilograms) of lead, the box was thrown from a tugboat into New York's harbor. In less than a minute, Houdini was free. When sailors pulled the box back up, it was still nailed shut with the manacles inside.

manacle— to bind someone's hands and feet with metal cuffs and chains

A Mysterious Injury

On October 22, 1926, three college students visited Houdini backstage in Montreal, Quebec, Canada. One of them asked if he could test Houdini's strength by punching Houdini in the stomach—a common challenge. Houdini agreed. Before the magician could brace his stomach muscles, the student delivered three hard blows. He didn't mean to hurt Houdini, and Houdini claimed he felt fine afterwards.

A few days later, however, Houdini began to feel ill. In Detroit, Michigan, he was so sick his manager wanted to cancel the performance. Houdini refused. He wowed the crowd, as usual, but collapsed the minute the curtain. Shortly thereafter, Houdini died in a hospital. Doctors said his appendix had burst.

United States' Famous Magic Shops

Harry Potter may have found his wand at Ollivander's, but Houdini shopped at Martinka's! He even owned it for a while. Located in New Jersey, Martinka's is still open today.

So what was the *first* magic shop in the United States? Magic historians believe it was Hartz's Magical Repository. Gus and Joseph Hartz opened the shop on Broadway in New York in 1869.

The Broken Wand

Harry Houdini died on October 31, 1926. Thousands attended his funeral on November 4. Every year the Society of American Magicians holds its Broken Wand ceremony at his grave in Queens, New York.

Abracadabra to Sim Sala Bim!

Where Do Magic Words Come From?

Where would magic be without "hocus-pocus," "open sesame," or presto chango"? Some of these words are taken from folklore and foreign languages. Others are just made up. Can you match these six with their sources?

1. Abracadabra!

2. Hocus-pocus!

3. Open sesame!

4. Presto chango!

5. Voila!

6. Shazam!

a. a mix of Italian and English meaning "quick change!"

b. what Ali Baba said to open the magic cave in "Ali Baba and the Forty Thieves," a story from *The Arabian Nights*

c. the title of the first illustrated book in the English language devoted entirely to the subject of magic

d. French for "See here!" It is often used after a trick to accentuate the moment.

e. a word believed to be based on an ancient Roman **amulet** using the Hebrew alphabet

f. a word that was adopted from the 1940s comic book character Captain Marvel

Answers: 1 e; 2 c; 3 b; 4 a; 5 d; 6 f

Chapter 4

America's Royal Dynasty and Beyond

The Kings of Magic

The United States may be a democracy, but magic still has royalty! The Mantle of the Royal Dynasty of Magic represents a series of tricks or set of props passed down from one master magician to another. How did this dynasty begin?

Explosive Beginnings

In 1858, 9 year-old Harry Kellar started working in a pharmacy. He loved to conduct secret experiments with chemicals. When young Kellar blew a hole in the shop's floor, he knew he needed to find another job. Kellar answered an ad for a magician's assistant and was soon performing shows on his own. He called himself "Kellar the Wizard" and excelled at cutting off his own head.

FACT:
Harry Kellar's real name was Heinrich Keller until 1911, when he legally changed it to "Harry Kellar."

The Royal Dynasty

- Harry Kellar
- Howard Thurston
- Dante
- Lee Grabel
- Lance Burton

ONE OF **THURSTON'S** ASTOUNDING MYSTERIES

SHE FLOATS ALL OVER THE STAGE AND INTO THE AUDIENCE, THEN VANISHES LIKE A FADING CLOUD

Lee Grabel passed the Mantle of Magic to Lance Burton on May 12, 1994.

The Saga Continues

After performing for nearly 50 years, Kellar retired in 1908. In a grand ceremony, Kellar passed on his cape and props to fellow magician, Howard Thurston. Magicians began referring to Kellar's things as the "Mantle of Magic," and thus the Royal Dynasty was born.

Thurston

Howard Thurston was one of the greatest **prestidigitators**, or sleight of hand artists, ever known. One of Thurston's best tricks was The Back Palm, in which he made cards disappear. How did he do it? In basic terms, he flipped the card backward behind his hand with two fingers, then held it there. When he opened his palm to the audience, the card was gone! It is a difficult trick, but practice makes perfect.

Dante

After Thurston died in 1936, the Mantle of Magic passed to Harry Jansen, also called Dante. That same year, Dante opened his traveling magic show, *Sim Sala Bim!* What did the words mean? Nothing. But audiences loved how it sounded. Dante was also among the first magicians to perform on TV, the new "magic medium" of the 1950s.

prestidigitation—magic tricks using rapid hand work

The Magic Detective

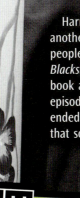

Harry Blackstone Sr. was another master magician. Most people knew him as the star of *Blackstone, the Magic Detective*, a comic book and radio series of the 1940s. Each episode posed a puzzle to the audience and ended with an explanation of the magic trick that solved it.

FACT: When Harry Blackstone Sr. died in 1965, his son donated many of his props to the Smithsonian Museum. Among them was a floating light bulb Thomas Edison made just for Blackstone's act.

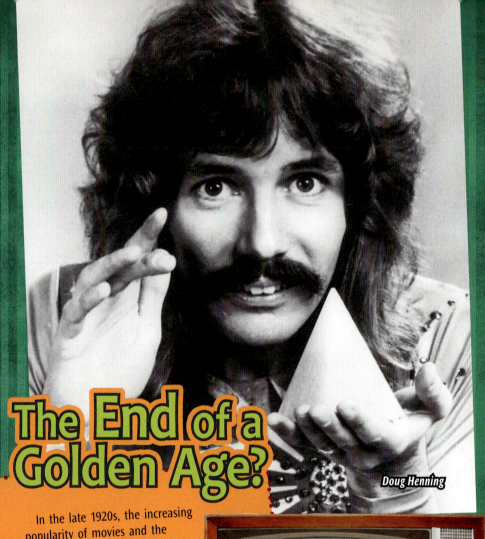

The End of a Golden Age?

Doug Henning

In the late 1920s, the increasing popularity of movies and the start of the Great Depression (1929–1939) took some of the shine off magic. In the following years, many magicians migrated from theaters to smaller nightclubs, with just a few making a break on TV.

Mark Wilson hosted his own show called *Magic Land of Allakazam*. Later he had a TV series called *Magic Circus*.

Two of the United States most popular and important magicians during the 1960s, 1970s, and early 1980s were Mark Wilson and Doug Henning.

Doug Henning breathed life back into TV magic in the 1970s by taking a new approach. He cast aside stuffy tuxedos to present magic wearing simple jeans and T-shirts or colorful 70s fashions. His illusions were full of color, wonder, and the realm of fantasy.

FACT: During one of Henning's live TV specials, the tigers used in one of his illusions escaped backstage and went on a rampage! Henning was forced to stop live TV shows and moved to pre-recorded shows only.

Queens of Magic

Magic has had its queens as well as its kings. Adelaide Herrmann (1853–1932) started out as an assistant to her husband, the magician Alexander Herrmann. When he died in 1896, she took over his act. Most people at that time believed a woman couldn't be an expert magician. Adelaide soon proved them wrong.

On January 19, 1897, she performed the dangerous bullet catch trick. She became known as the "Queen of Magic" and continued to tour until she was 75.

Dell O'Dell (1902–1962) learned her early routines from her father, a circus performer. She wrote several souvenir booklets about magic for her fans and often gave them away at her performances.

In 1988, Dorothy Dietrich successfully performed the bullet catch trick in Atlantic City, New Jersey. She is such an accomplished "escapologist" that her fans call her "the female Houdini."

Today more than 500 women belong to the Academy of Magical Arts. One of the most popular is Fanny Tjin, or Jade, of San Francisco. Her tricks include a rice bowl that doubles its contents and dancing butterflies that appear out of thin air. In 1990, she won one of magic's highest awards, the Gold Medal from the International Brotherhood of Magicians (IBM). Jade's award proved that the brotherhood is now a sisterhood too.

FACT:
The IBM has more than 300 clubs, called Rings, located in more than 30 countries. Founded in 1922, the IBM is the world's largest organization for professional and amateur magicians.

THE INTERNATIONAL BROTHERHOOD OF MAGICIANS
I·B·M

Chapter 5

Magic Meets the 21st Century

David Copperfield

In 1968, 12-year-old David became the youngest person ever admitted to the Society of American Magicians.

Born David Kotkin in 1956, he claimed he had learned magic because he was shy and wanted to make friends. It worked.

DAVID COPPERFIELD
CHARLES DICKENS   Vol. I

COLLECTION

At 16, he taught a course in magic at New York University. Two years later he took the stage name "David Copperfield" from the book by Charles Dickens. He felt that, like Dickens' character, he overcame many obstacles to reach his goal.

Copperfield is one of the best-known magicians today and performs in sold-out arenas around the world.

On April 8, 1983, millions of TV viewers couldn't believe their eyes. Before a live audience, David Copperfield made the Statue of Liberty vanish, then reappear. How did he do it? All we can say is that it's a secret that revolves around your point of view.

FACT: In 1982, David Copperfield brought "Project Magic" to California's Freeman Memorial Hospital. Project Magic helps disabled people develop coordination and confidence through learning basic magic tricks.

David Blaine
Making the Magic Connection

David Blaine was born in Brooklyn, New York, on April 4, 1973. Some of his first tricks were performed with his grandmother's Tarot cards. The cards, he said, made his tricks seem even more mysterious.

While performing street magic in New York's Greenwich Village, Blaine asks a homeless man if he can look at his cup of hot coffee. When Blaine shakes the cup, the coffee disappears, and the cup overflows with coins.

In addition to his street magic, Blaine performs stunts to test his physical endurance. In 2006, he spent seven days submerged in a water-filled glass sphere while breathing through a tube. This feat put him in the *Guinness Book of World Records*.

As part of his street magic performances, David Blaine asks to borrow a boy's baseball cap. He presents the empty cap to the crowd, then reaches inside. The crowd gasps as Blaine pulls a live snake out of the hat.

Blaine has performed all over the world, from the White House to remote villages in the South American rain forest. Magic, he says, is all about connecting to people. "If there's no connection," he told an *LA Times* reporter, "there's no magic."

FACT: In January 2010 in New York's Times Square, Blaine performed magic tricks non-stop for 72 hours. His magic marathon raised money for the victims of a recent earthquake in Haiti.

Super Freak

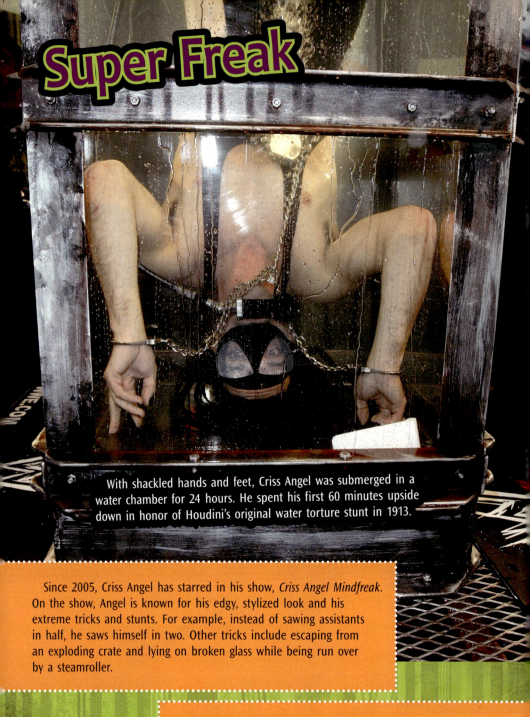

With shackled hands and feet, Criss Angel was submerged in a water chamber for 24 hours. He spent his first 60 minutes upside down in honor of Houdini's original water torture stunt in 1913.

Since 2005, Criss Angel has starred in his show, *Criss Angel Mindfreak*. On the show, Angel is known for his edgy, stylized look and his extreme tricks and stunts. For example, instead of sawing assistants in half, he saws himself in two. Other tricks include escaping from an exploding crate and lying on broken glass while being run over by a steamroller.

Angel not only loves his fans but listens to them. On *Mindfreak*'s second season, he made a 9,000-pound (4,082-kilogram) Asian elephant named Thai disappear. After the show aired, he received dozens of letters from concerned children who knew that Thai belonged to an endangered species. The next season, he made Thai reappear to show the kids she was alive and well.

PLATFORM 9¾

Can Your Mind Work Magic?

In 2004, Scott Hamel of Albany, New York, made a cursor jump across a monitor without a mouse, voice command, or keyboard. He moved the cursor simply by thinking about it. Hamel was one of several volunteers at the University of New York's Wadsworth Center for the Study of Nervous System Disorders. To accomplish the feat, Hamel wore a special cap that could sense his brain signals.

This isn't magic. It's science. But magic and science are not always opposites. The magician and the scientist are both interested in exploring the limits of what we can understand. They both encourage us to sharpen wits, think twice about what we see, and look at the world in a whole new way.

TIMELINE

ANCIENT AND MEDIEVAL

2170 BC — Egyptian scribe records the story of Dedi the Pharaoh's magician.

135 BC — Greek soldier Eunios frightens enemies with his fire-breathing trick.

1133 AD — Saint Bartholomew's Day Fair is founded in England by Rahere, the juggling monk.

1584 AD — *Discovery of Witchcraft* by Reginald Scot, the first book with a chapter on performance magic, is published.

MODERN

1845 — Jean Eugene Robert-Houdin opens the world's first theater for magic in Paris, France.

1893 — Eric Weiss changes his name to Harry Houdini and begins performing magic on Coney Island.

1897 — Adelaide Herrmann becomes the first woman to successfully perform the bullet catch trick.

1908 — Harry Kellar retires and gives his props, known as the Mantle of Magic, to Howard Thurston, thus starting the American Dynasty of Magic.

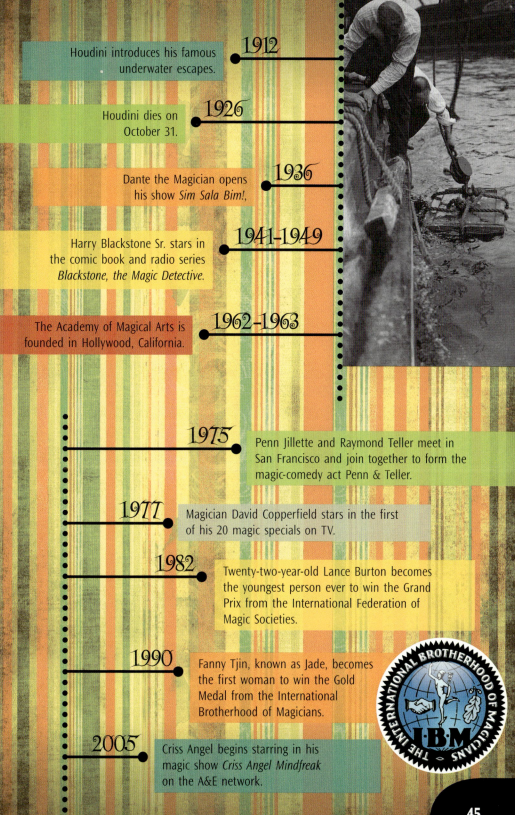

1912 — Houdini introduces his famous underwater escapes.

1926 — Houdini dies on October 31.

1936 — Dante the Magician opens his show *Sim Sala Bim!*,

1941–1949 — Harry Blackstone Sr. stars in the comic book and radio series *Blackstone, the Magic Detective*.

1962–1963 — The Academy of Magical Arts is founded in Hollywood, California.

1975 — Penn Jillette and Raymond Teller meet in San Francisco and join together to form the magic-comedy act Penn & Teller.

1977 — Magician David Copperfield stars in the first of his 20 magic specials on TV.

1982 — Twenty-two-year-old Lance Burton becomes the youngest person ever to win the Grand Prix from the International Federation of Magic Societies.

1990 — Fanny Tjin, known as Jade, becomes the first woman to win the Gold Medal from the International Brotherhood of Magicians.

2005 — Criss Angel begins starring in his magic show *Criss Angel Mindfreak* on the A&E network.

THE INTERNATIONAL BROTHERHOOD OF MAGICIANS · IBM

GLOSSARY

amulet (AM-yoo-let)—a small charm or object said to ward off evil or bring good luck

automaton (ah-TAH-muh-tahn)—a robot or mechanical figure made to resemble a person or animal

conjure (KON-juhr)—to do something by magic

levitate (LEH-vi-tate)—to rise in the air and float

manacle (MAN-uh-kul)—to bind someone's hands and feet with metal cuffs and chains

prestidigitation (pres-tuh-dij-uh-TAY-shuhn)—magic tricks using rapid hand work, also known as sleight of hand

props (PROPS)—objects used in a performance that can be carried on or off the stage

sleight of hand (SLAIT UV HAND)—a quick, cleverly performed trick or deception

straitjacket (STRAYT-jak-it)—a jacket with long sleeves that can be tied behind the wearer's back as a form of restraint

supernatural (soo-pur-NACH-ur-uhl)—something that cannot be explained by science or logic

READ MORE

Barnhart, Norm. *Amazing Magic Tricks.* Mankato, Minn.: Capstone Press, 2008.

Burgess, Ron. *Kids Make Magic!: The Complete Guide to Becoming an Amazing Magician.* Charlotte, Vt.: Williamson Pub., 2004.

Carlson, Laurie. *Harry Houdini for Kids: His Life and Adventures with 21 Magic Tricks and Illusions.* For Kids. Chicago: Chicago Review Press, 2009.

INTERNET SITES

FactHound offers a safe, fun way to find Internet sites related to this book. All of the sites on FactHound have been researched by our staff.

Here's all you do:

Visit *www.facthound.com*

Type in this code: 9781429647915

INDEX